"The strength to endure with Grace"
Psalm 1:3

Life of **JOY**
The Key to Transformed Living

QuiNina J. Sinceno

Edited by: Iantha C. Ussin & Casandra Lott-Woods

Life of JOY: The Key to Transformed Living

Copyright © 2016 by QuiNina J. Sinceno
Self-Published by QuiNina J. Sinceno
GDI Enterprises
Destrehan, LA

Printed in the United States of America

All rights reserved worldwide. No part of this book may be reproduced, stored in a retrieval system, or transmitted in any form or by any means, for example, electronic, mechanical, photocopy, or recording without prior written permission of the publisher. The only exception is brief cited quotations in printed reviews.

Unless otherwise noted, all scripture quotations and references or mentions are from the New King James or Amplified Versions of the Bible.

DEDICATION

Dear Parents,

The greatest gift parents can give to their child is an introduction to Jesus Christ. Thank you for giving me the greatest gift a child could ever receive.

Dear Spiritual Parents and Mentors,

Oftentimes you are the ones who help us to grow and mature beyond the fears and setbacks of previous generations. Thank you for pushing me into an awareness of greatness within.

Dear Family & Friends,

Thank you for being just who you are, family!

CONTENTS

PREFACE

INTRODUCTION: Hello, My Name is Joy

- ONE. The Seed of Joy
- TWO. Prayer is Your Fertilizer
- THREE. Watering Your Seed
- FOUR. Process of Growth
- FIVE. The Root of Joy is Faith
- SIX. The Branches of Joy
- SEVEN. The Fruit of Joy
- EIGHT. Harvesting What's Yours

ABOUT THE AUTHOR: Affected Lives and Their Stories

FOREWORD
AFFECTED LIVES, THEIR STORY

Also now, behold my witness is in heaven, and my record is on high. John 16:19

I am not sure what year it was, but I do remember where it was; New Living Word Ministries in Ruston, Louisiana. My first recollection of her was of her on the praise team. She stood out among the few who stood their praising God and leading the congregation. Every Sunday it seemed she was different but yet the same (a true worshipper) and different in outward appearance but consistent in her desire to press through to that Holy place. One Sunday she would "rock" a pair of jeans and t-shirt, the next a model's runway outfit and the next a preppy college girl and the next a "first lady" outfit. Those two things seemed to have drawn me to her: A free spirit, not conformed, not perfect, not trying to pretend to be, just plain ole QuiNina. Well, I shouldn't say just or plain to describe her because nothing is "just" or "plain" about her.

I was teaching the Women's ministry and she was faithful in attendance and in challenging me and the other women in growing. We developed a wonderful friendship over the years that included laughing a lot, playing basketball, playing chess, collaborating on women's conferences that transformed lives, awesome prayer meetings, and so much more. Unlike many friendships she and I had a rule, unspoken but agreed upon, that if planned anything at a given time and the other one did not show up as agreed we left; No explanations, or questions about why you did not wait. She beat me at basketball and I beat her at chess, but we together won many for Christ. We grew so close that she actually moved into my home, fondly known as The House of Hope, for a summer. She is younger enough to be my daughter yet wise enough to be my confidant and friend. I've watched her mature and press through very difficult times, but she'd made look easy. She refused to take on the daughter role although she respected me and the call on my life; she knew her position was to serve in another role. Often when I talked about some idea too long she would put fire under my behind and blast or catapult me into the place of destiny. I loved then and I still do love it. During the past seven or eight years we have connected on so many levels. I remember when I went to Africa for the first time; QuiNina was a true champion to assist me in getting there. She said then, "I am going one day," and she did. She graduated from college amid some very difficult physical struggles. She has accomplished so much, but relative to what is left inside of her she has done so little. She is so packed with potential that it is bursting into reality. Look out world!

But there is a part of our relationship nobody knows, but I want to share. In 2006, when my mother and best friend (the same person) was dying of lung cancer QuiNina was the friend ONLY God could have given me. There were some very unpleasant dynamics among me and my siblings. The last two nights of my mother's life QuiNina spent the night at the hospital with me. I shall never forget that. I know she was there praying for me, my family, and of course my mother. She watched me face the most difficult times I have ever faced, she watched me be the daughter I hoped would make God and my mother proud, she watched me and stood by me as I grew as a woman.

A few years later God would position me to watch her face some totally different but most definitely difficult times. She shared with me some of her difficulties physically. I remember I watched her body change right before my eyes. Because of the depth of our friendship, we shared liberties that many people do not have in typical friendships. Not sure the outcome I ventured into a candid conversation about what I observed about her physically. I told her that I observed her eyes drooping, speech slurred, and the difficulty she was having lifting her legs in out of the vehicle. A lot was transpiring in both our lives, but we managed to get her to my physician and he told her what he believed to be the problem. And that she needed to immediately get to the hospital. We managed to get over to LSU Shreveport as that was where he suggested we go because of the nature of the problem. We finally made it there and it was there that it was confirmed that my physician was medically on the right track. That was the beginning of this remarkable journey of courage and faith in walking out God's word regarding healing, and being whole as I have witnessed in the life of my friend. One miracle after another; I remember her saying you are the only one who has said that to me, and I was supposed to be THAT one like she was to be THAT one for me during those last days with my mother. We candidly talk about life, and what matters. I am so thankful for this JOY that God has brought in my life. She's a confronter, comforter, confidant, and collaborator for the building of God's kingdom. Everyone needs a little Joy. QuiNina is truly a rare treasure, a warrior, a worshipper, and woman of God. Thank you for allowing me to be a part of this journey of faith and triumph. I want you to dance at my wedding.

Love you,
Lili, C. Alisa Greene
Author, Moma's Gone Now What

I have had the privilege of being friends with QuiNina Sinceno for over 11 years now. As a result of our friendship, I was introduced to my husband, Vincent Brown. Our friendship was birthed as a result of Hurricane Katrina. I was serving as a case manager for Volunteers of America and QuiNina was one of my clients. Through the process of serving as her case manager, we developed not only a friendship but we also became co-laborers in spreading the Gospel of Jesus Christ. We had the opportunity to work together in many ministerial capacities such as street ministry, television ministry, campus ministry, Christian conferences and mission work in Africa. QuiNina has such a commitment to God and Kingdom Business.

Her commitment and trust in God have sustained her through major physical challenges. Through QuiNina's life, I have seen her defeat death by the Grace of God several times. Her determination to live and not die has caused her to be motivation to a countless number of people. QuiNina's life has been an inspiration of endurance, faith, hope, courage and integrity. QuiNina Sinceno is a true testimony of the Goodness of God.

Dr. Lorie Hopkins-Brown
Pastor, Liberty Christian Center West

Galatians 6:9 reads, "And let us not be weary in well doing: for in due season we shall reap, if we faint not." Our present time is seed time and I must ask what have you sown? Seed time brings the believer's life great "Joy," partially because we know that we can't deceive nature any more than we can fool God. Don't be deceived it's your sowing that produces a harvest! What will you reap in due season?

I am honored to be able to watch and experience Minister QuiNina Sinceno reap the harvest of her sowing. Much like a farmer, she sowed patience, strength, endurance, and resilience during some of the toughest moments of her life. I can remember sitting in my living room and listening to her as she spoke and testified to the goodness of Jesus and all that He had done for her. She shared how she had to encourage herself in the Lord when there was no one else around to encourage her. Yet, her words affirmed that she knew in due season or at the right time the harvest would come.

I celebrate and praise God with her, as she continues to experience and enjoy the newness that God has blessed her with during this season. May the Joy of the Lord be her strength, as her dreams, passions, and desires sprout forth into a mighty harvest.

Minister Casandra Lott-Woods

Potters House of Dallas, TX

All I knew was I wanted to be used by God. I'd been in a relationship with Christ for about two years and the Word of God and His principles were my breath of life. I was seeking Him with my whole heart, desperate for opportunities to minister His word to young women and girls and teach them how to walk as women of God. He fed my hunger.

God gave me, a third-year student on a very liberal college campus, a crafty design for a women's bible study. That crafty design drew many young women to the initial gathering, but the Holy Spirit spoke gently to me and said that I was to disciple QuiNina. And so it was. That day, she became mine.

She had friends, but she was a "stand out" in her crew. She'd be with them, but she was never really there. She was a part of a loving family, but the relationship was broken and she did not feel loved, thus her disdain. She smiled, but she wanted a new smile. That smile she had was one that she was accustomed to putting on to keep passersby from "seeing" her. God had me to see her though, and I saw beyond what others were able to see. He showed me her heart and how she wanted to be free—free to revisit past hurts and be healed, regardless of what others may think; free to break away from unfruitful relationships and stand completely alone in Christ if she had to; free to be exactly who God created her to be, with no shame, no regrets, and no apologies.

The first two years of discipleship was a breaking ground. We spent time in the word in the bible study with other young women, and we spent time in the word apart from the study, one on one. We prayed together; we traveled together; we ate together; we fellowshipped together. God had me to show her, literally, what it meant to live for Him in every area of life. Her heart was hungry to walk in the ways of God, so the breaking was easy and the rebuilding was too.

A new QuiNina surfaced—a QuiNina who loved God and His word with an undeniable intensity. A prayer warrior took post. As a seer, she opened her eyes. A life had been transformed for the kingdom!

And just as Jesus called his disciples and taught them what it meant to call others into the kingdom, and just as He later called them His friends because of the nature of their relationship, my relationship with QuiNina, after all of our heart to hearts and our work together in ministry, transformed from discipleship to friendship.

It has been one of the most fulfilling relationships of my life. We have since prayed together, cried together, served God's people together, ministered to the lost together... We have watched each other fail and lifted each other up. We have seen each other through many firsts and closed doors on many of each other's lasts. We have taken road trips just to talk and came out refreshed after having had that time together. When I started my business, a trip across four states was no question for her, and when sickness attacked her body, a trip across four states was no question for me. We are truly sisters in Christ, and our love for each other runs deep.

And it runs deep because QuiNina loves deep. She has a heart for true, God-breathed relationship with people, so she prayerfully fosters those relationships. She wants to see God's people free and living on purpose, so she showers them with God's love until they reach freedom. She wants people to know that when they have Christ, they can have joy in pain, so she speaks openly about God's ability to heal physical, emotional, and spiritual pain. Her transformed life is a testimony to behold, and the pages of this book are sure to inspire you to live on purpose knowing that no matter what comes, you too, with Christ, can have a *Life of Joy*!

Iantha Ussin
Praise Movement School of Dance, LLC

PREFACE
LIFE OF JOY

Hello. I'd like to begin our journey together with an introduction, not of myself, but of the greater one, Jesus Christ, if you have yet to meet Him. Meeting Him has been the greatest encounter I have ever had, and I am sure there will be no greater encounter in the future. He rescued me from my sins long before I was born by choosing to accept His Father's will by giving himself as a ransom for my redemption. He died on a cross just for me, and He also died just for you. There is no greater love than the love of Jesus Christ. He loved us so that He rose from the dead, giving us the opportunity to have eternal life, if we choose to accept Him as our Lord and Savior.

I pray you have accepted Christ into your heart, and if you haven't, great! I stopped to write this section just for you. It is as simple as ABC to receive this same gift into your heart; it is the gift of everlasting life and forgiveness from all sins. Just confess with your mouth and believe in your heart that God raised Jesus from the dead for the remission of your sins, accept your forgiveness and that is it! You are saved! Welcome to the family of God!

Secondly, thank you for taking the time to invest into transforming your life into a life of JOY. Even if you are currently experiencing a life of JOY, there is something within this book that can take that life of JOY and shift it to an even greater level. A level of being one who aids in transforming lives by transferring the Joy of the Lord to those you come in contact with. We, the saints of God, have a responsibility to display the Joy of the Lord to the world. Sadly, we have not done as great of a job as we should. My prayer is for that to change and it is going to begin with you and me. Before we get a little deeper into the subject, let's begin this journey with a clear understanding.

What Is Joy?

Many times we associate joy with a feeling or an emotion that is pleasant or delightful as a result of an event that has taken place. We typically deem joy to be something internal that comes and goes. That, however, is the secular perspective of joy; it is not the way God describes Joy in His Word. The joy of the world is a feeling or emotion, but the joy of the Lord is a substance produced by your faith. It is your strength. It is an everlasting assurance that all things work together for good because you love God and are called according to His purpose, which brings about a peace that produces the power to relieve all stress, anger, pain, and anxiety. Therefore, living a life of Joy metaphorically means living a life of Strength, because if we can possess the Joy of the Lord, we then possess the God kind of Strength that empowers us to endure with grace victoriously.

Joy is also a fruit of the spirit of God, meaning that the spirit of God supplies you with a substance to feed on, which is its fruit. Not only does this fruit of the spirit allow you to feast on it, it also holds seeds within it to plant the potential for such a fruit to grow within others, creating a cycle of transferring and multiplying JOY into the lives of others.

When I started the journey of writing this book I wanted to make sure that it was not just an average book that tells you of someone's story. Though testimonies are quite encouraging when read I felt telling you the bulk of my story would be of no benefit to you if by the close of the book nothing was imparted for the enhancement of your life. Therefore, I have attempted to intentionally not give you the chronological standard testimony of my journey, but instead, I seek to give you what I have learned along the way through my experiences and processes as it relates to living a life of Joy. I believe giving someone else the tools needed to successfully live a life of Joy through sharing what I've learned behind the story makes surviving through the season of testimony worthwhile.

INTRODUCTION
HELLO, MY NAME IS JOY

Can you imagine a twenty-five year old at the prime of her life? She is seemingly a picture of perfect health; a beautiful young athletic woman of a decent weight because she's running three miles a day. A jazzy girl who is holding down three jobs in the zesty city of New Orleans, full of dreams and visions for starting her own businesses one day, she hopes of a better life, has a delightful relationship with her creator, God, a desire to fulfill His purpose for her life, and is active in ministry. Then all of a sudden, it changes in just a few moments. She starts to feel different; her body has become fatigued, and then one day it decides to completely shut down and she no longer has control of any of her extremities. Her heart and lungs have decided to take a break, leaving her threateningly lifeless. After weeks of intubation and a series of extensive tests, the doctors decide to narrow down their diagnosis to a neurological muscular dystrophy that is said to be incurable. They offered an estimated life expectancy based on the severity of her condition compared to previous research studies as well as experiences. They also suggested an emergency surgery that could possibly later cause her to go into remission if the surgery was successful. At that moment, she remained optimistic and positive, believing that she would somehow receive an instant miracle and wake up, and it would be all over; she could return back to the life she was building before...

Well, it hasn't quite happened that way since the diagnosis in 2009, but I am still fighting. There have been times when I have totally wanted to give up because I felt as though there was nothing left in me to fight with or fight for. Who would have thought that at the age of twenty-five I would be entering an extensively intense season of fighting for my life? Definitely not me! I cannot accurately say it is the fight of my life because I believe I am too young to release such words and have decades of living ahead of me that I have yet to discover. But, I can say that this particular fight was a fight like none other. Nevertheless, through that I have learned what true JOY is and the strength that it bears. *Getting to the point of living life free of depression and oppression in the midst of an ongoing crisis has become one of my most precious possessions.* I pray that sharing with you the process of achieving such through my experiences transforms your life so that you too are able to handle anything that may come your way with grace.

Little did I know that the things I learned previously through hard times and challenging circumstances were the very things that established the true substance of my character and would be required of me through "show and tell."

Our true nature always reveals itself during challenges

Thankfully, early on, I had already made a decision to continuously enhance my relationship with God before I entered this particular fight. I did not know what was ahead, but looking back, all of those days of fasting, early mornings of prayer, and nights that I would sit up reading my Bible or listening to gospel music as I sang along in worship, have now revealed themselves to be my moments of preparation. Those moments planted the seeds of eternal Joy into my spirit and soul before I reached my season of testing because I chose to be open to receive the seeds God provided. Without knowing what type of trees or fruit they would produce *I just ate.*

Many times, because our thoughts are consumed by our present, the thought of maybe being prepared for something much larger ahead never crosses our minds. *It is almost as though our moments of what may actually be our practice test is seen in our eyes as the final exam. We tend to lack the foresight that our present is currently attempting to equip us for what is ahead along the way.* Realizing a situation has attempted to enhance your life can oftentimes be revolutionary if you allow wisdom to fulfill its purpose. Looking back in an "ahh-ha" manner makes you realize all things really do work together for good to them that love God. The assurance that God's word never lies and an unshakeable belief in such is the strongest foundation of faith and joy one could possess, but it takes development.

Just as a seed must be planted into the ground to grow, so should God's word be planted into your heart to produce a life of JOY.

Let's start digging, shall we?

ONE
THE SEED OF JOY

It is the spirit that quickens; the flesh profits nothing: the words that I speak unto you, they are spirit, and they are life. John 6:63

Anytime there is a life form that is about to surface, there will always be some type of seed that has been planted to produce that life form. For example, when we want flowers we plant a seed into the ground, and when we want to conceive a child a male plants a seed into a woman, and life begins.

It works the same way spiritually. When we develop a greater desire for our relationship with Christ to become a living testimony, we then must first plant the seed. *That seed that must be planted is the Word of God-the life source that activates and empowers the soil of our hearts.*

Purpose of Planting

We plant the Word of God into the soil of our hearts through generally two or three ways: reading and studying the scriptures in the Bible, by hearing rhema (an utterance from the Holy Spirit which speaks directly to you or your current state) through sermons preached by men and women of God, or by fellowship. In some cases "iron sharpens iron." This entails a meaningful fellowship of believers who build each other up in faith by holding each other accountable to their beliefs and convictions based on the Word of God. Such fellowship is for the sole purpose of becoming stronger. Adding people to your circle who are Godly and astute in the Word of God can richly enhance your life and aid in your maturity as a believer. There is always a greater level of strength in numbers vs being a lone ranger. Throughout the scriptures the Word teaches us of strength that numbers can bring.

Importance of the Soil

The life of the seed is contingent upon the purity of the soil. Bad soil or a lack thereof can choke, contaminate, or kill the seed planted. Thus, the soil of your heart is your most valuable asset because it determines the potential and potency of the seed.

Your soil directly affects your seed's ability to grow into its purpose with strength.

Atmosphere vs Environment

Soil represents your atmosphere. It provides your seed with nourishment. Your ability to remain in a nourished atmosphere is dependent upon your environment. Now I know that the two are often considered to have the same meaning but I suggest to you that there is a fine line between atmosphere and environment, which, in fact, makes them different. Let me explain. According to Webster, the atmosphere is defined as the air of locality. In other words, atmosphere is the air in a particular place or area. Environment is defined as the aggregate of social and cultural conditions that influence the life of an individual or community, or in other words, the conditions that surround someone or something. It is my belief according to personal studies and experiences that atmosphere is far more important than environment. Yes, environment plays a part, but your atmosphere, your air, the substance that provides you with the ability to breathe properly, carries much more weight. I am a firm believer that there can be two individuals growing up in a relatively hostile environment but in two different atmospheres and turn out completely different. We see it sometimes in our neighborhoods, there may be a kid who grew up in a poverty-stricken environment, but because his atmosphere was an atmosphere of wealth (meaning love, respect, morals, and the presence of God) he still became successful in life. He may have had someone around to make sure he went to school or completed his homework on time and stayed out of trouble. Just an encourager of some sort present to reach towards, rather than allowing the environment to contain and restrict who he could become compared to his classmate next door whose home was the complete opposite, leaving him too often to have to fend for himself.

Your atmosphere is what you take in; it is what you inhale. But your environment is your container. Though containers create restrictions or limitations they are not permanent. When a substance inside of a container has out grown the container it almost always causes the container to break or overwhelms the container, causing an overflow. Therefore, your environment is only the limitation that you allow it to be. Ultimately it is what is in you that will prevail. It is your choice to grow within or not, as well as, how much you choose to expand beyond the environment that you choose to expand beyond.

Matters of the Heart

Maintaining healthy, productive, consistency in your atmosphere guarantees the nourishment needed for your heart. A healthy consistency in your environment is an added bonus but your atmosphere is most important. The condition of your heart determines your ability to receive nourishment for stability. What that means is your Joy is dependent upon the ability of your heart to allow the word of God to take root. Thus, a heart that wavers is a heart that is unstable and easily broken. This explains why the seed of the Word of God is often lost or looks as though the Word taught is no longer present in one's life. One moment a person may believe, and the next they may not. Part of that problem is because of a wavering heart, which prevents the seed of the

Word of God from sticking or staying in place. It doesn't take root. Remember, the state of your heart dictates the atmosphere of your environment.

To begin to foster a life of joy a seed must first be planted into an atmosphere that can be nourished by the soil. The nourishment of the seed is highly dependent upon the soil because it is the soil that filters a substance to the seed. Thus, the richness of the soil determines its ability to nourish; a heart with a desire for the Word of God will create an environment to produce a healthy seed of Joy. When our hearts are hearts of love and purity, we increase in richness (potency) and ability to handle being planted into by, or receive from God. It is our responsibility to make sure the atmosphere of our heart does not filter toxins into our seed. We must be mindful of how we conduct ourselves and the way we treat others. Allowing our character to be corrupt can drastically affect our seed. Another way to look at it is this: picture a pregnant mother. The baby is the seed. It is her responsibility to make sure she pays attention to what she eats or ingests into her body because it affects the growth of her child. It is unhealthy for her baby if she allows herself to be around smoke or consumes alcohol. It is the same way spiritually. We must protect the seed of the Word of God that is in our hearts.

> *We cannot continuously surround ourselves with the smog of sin and expect for the Word in us to breathe life into our situations.*

A rocky heart, one that is full of anger, or a stony heart, one that harvests unforgiveness, prevents the growth of the seed. It prevents the Word of God from continuing to grow in your life. Holding grudges and strife chokes the life out of the seed of the Word that has been planted in your heart.

Unforgiveness is your heart's enemy. *You have to make sure that your heart has been softened and the soil is rich and ready to receive the seed of the Word because the potential of your life of JOY depends on it.*

Let's Reflect

I can remember a time when I was ill; I used to be so angry and hurt during those moments of feeling neglected. At that time I needed friends or family members however they never showed up for me physically. There were many times when I would have to be put on a ventilator to breathe and those who I felt like I'd done the most for never returned the same effort when it came down to expressing their concern for my well-being. But God never left me. He would always send unexpected blessings to look after me, whether it was a praying nurse or a fellow sister in Christ. Most times it was usually always someone different.

I had to learn how to guard my heart, release the hurt, anger, unforgiveness, and bitterness. After all, it was only affecting me; everyone else was busy with their normal lives, oblivious to my hurt and disappointment. Just for a moment, I allowed myself to be stagnated, by not providing the right soil; I was hindering the rich soil of the Word to be planted in my own life. The atmosphere of my heart was infecting the environment of my seed and its ability to receive the healing nourishment of the Word of God.

The Choice

Real living begins when we begin to allow the Word of God to take its rightful position in our lives. The Word of God changes everything; it goes into the deep places of our hearts to position our lives to begin to be fulfilling and purposeful. It changes our thinking from one form or commonality to the way of the kingdom. We no longer think, respond, or perceive as we once did while in the world, but because we are now new in Christ, we allow the word to cause us to have the mind of Christ, thinking according to the system and ways of the Kingdom of Heaven.

The Word of God has the ability, if allowed, to renew your mind. Renewal controls your thoughts and ultimately your actions. Most reactions or actions are a direct result of a thought. *Therefore, let the seed of the Word be planted into your heart through the renewal of your mind so that your thinking will begin to produce the life that God desires for you. The renewal of your mind will transform your life.*

This is why it is important to know the scripture; hide it in your heart! It is what we think in our hearts about ourselves that creates whom we become:

what we think is what we speak, and what we speak reflects our heart. I call this the *"cycle of the seed"*. Every seed produces after its own kind and the atmosphere that we create, along with the environments that we allow the states of our hearts to be in, directly affect or infect our ability to connect with the type of seed God has designed us to be.

Because the Words of God are spirit and are life, they are the first simple keys to nourishing your life. *When you speak the Word of God into your atmosphere, you create a divinely enriched environment.* **Remember you are what you eat.**

TWO
Prayer is Your Fertilizer

But we will give ourselves continually to prayer, and to the ministry of the word. Acts 6:4

Prayer, the secret weapon of the believer in Christ, can be accessed at any time and is encouraged to be used at all times. It is communication with our creator, God, in faith, petitioning, and thanksgiving through worship and praise. Prayer is one of the avenues to release all concerns, stresses, anguish, and discouragements to the One who hears and alleviates the heaviness that we may tend to take up on a daily basis. Not only that, but fervent prayer, wherever it is released activates the ability to transform the atmosphere to a place of peace.

You Must Push

Prayer brings our flesh under subjection by causing our minds and bodies to focus on God. The choice to center yourself to pray sets a priority in your life that begins to establish order in every other area. There will always be a reason not to pray. Every distraction known to man will often occur the moment you think you may want to begin to spend more time in prayer. That is because the enemy knows prayer is the key to unlocking every promise that has been held up, delayed, or detoured. Therefore, consistency is very beneficial but requires much discipline. Many times a consistent prayer life is a challenge because our flesh no longer has the control and isn't allowed to continue to be the determining factor of our responses and actions. We may want to stay in bed, may have other things that we feel require our attention and are "equally" important or the usual lack of motivation. If you have never developed a routine and have broken past the attempts placed before you initially-setting aside time for consistent prayer can be such a challenge because of the benefits that the enemy knows are available through prayer. That is why your flesh becomes so distracted when it is time for prayer. It is because the effective and fervent prayer of the righteous is quite dangerous to any opposition. Prayer has the power to strengthen, nourish, and grow the seed of the word within you in such a way that it manifests growth. It is the answer to the "dirty work" of a life of joy.

Dirty Work

The dirty work isn't what we run to when choosing tasks because oftentimes we are not publicly awarded, or no one is there to see us, so there is no praise, no "good jobs", or "keep up the good works" given. However, it must be done. Fertilizer is considered to be the nastiest part of the farming process because of the components within. But to fertilize means to make productive by adding suitable substances to it. Unfortunately, the "suitable substances" aren't always the most pleasant and comfortable additives to deal with. In life we go through things that are not pleasant; there are times when we'd like to give up. We may even give up at times because we feel as though we do not have the strength to continue to grow. Being constantly beaten, bruised, pushed, shoved, and kicked by life can really take a toll on our mental and emotion state at times. We can find ourselves in such unforgivingly dark places of despair through crushed dreams, broken hearts, and disappointments time and time again. Ever been there? If so, you may be going through fertilization. But do not worry everything is going to be ok, you'll grow through it.

It's Necessary

The fertilizer aids the soil in crushing the seed by breaking the shell so that the substance within can be released. In other words, it gives the Word of

God within you the opportunity to begin to grow in your life by being squeezed out through trials, adversity, tribulation, setbacks, challenges, and strife. During the pressure, it does not feel good at all, but it is definitely necessary! Fertilization must take place. The only way the seed can begin to grow and manifest as a living organism, is by going through the process of a type of crushing. The crushing process is not designed to kill the seed; it is not designed to diminish your faith or hinder your growth, but instead matures you for continual growth.

Consider it this way. When an individual who is out of shape decides they want to get into shape it takes a while before their routine becomes easier. First, it is a challenge to even make a decision to want to get into shape. Dissatisfaction must occur. Are you dissatisfied with not being able to reap from the benefits of prayer? Then along with making the decision to change other adjustments have to be made. Priorities have to be shifted based on how important getting into shape is for the individual. The adjustment always requires some type of sacrifice. Once the individual confronts the dissatisfaction, decides to change and shifts priorities, then the process of consistency begins as no planned workout days are missed. The first few times of working out are the absolute worse because certain muscles have not been stretched or used much so they become sore. However, this soreness is a good sign because it means the muscles are being worked. As time passes the activity that once caused your muscles to become sore is now a joy because strength has been built through discipline and consistency.

After a seed gets past the crushing stage, it has then proven itself to be unstoppable in becoming a life form. Your crushing process is designed to spark a life nourished by the Word of God in you. It is at this stage that the believer sees God as the healer, experiences God as the provider, recognizes God's presence as their peace, and it is revealed that in

God is everything that is needed. During the crushing process it is prayer that opens the channel for us to see and experience God for who He really is. Prayer provides the portal and produces the endurance for the dirty moments and the strength for the testing to come. Prayer has the ability to change the effects of the crushing process, meaning instead of situations causing a nervous breakdown or heart attack, prayer during crushing establishes character and incorporates your relationship with God as your safe haven. Prayer unto God enables healing when crushing seems to have allowed affliction. Yes it's a dirty part of the process but it's a must.

Though prayer is the secret weapon to enduring the crushing process of life and is the fertilizer of the seed of joy in our lives, this secret weapon comes with stipulations! Answered prayer comes with prerequisites such as: forgiving others, loving others and spouses correctly, repentance, and forgiveness of perpetual sin. These are personal hindrances that prevent prayers from being answered by God. For we are not to pray as the hypocrites do, who pray for self-gain and glory from a corrupt heart that breeds ulterior motives that do not honor the will of God.

Just as there are hindrances to prayer, there is also enhancement to prayer, an utterance given by the Holy Spirit, the third person of the trinity who is equally God. This utterance is also known as tongues or a heavenly language. This type of prayer from our spirits are words unknown to us but given to us, and spoken through us via the Holy Spirit who prays the perfect will of God, is just a stronger version of our secret weapon. It is freely given to all of those who receive.

[2]He said unto them, Have you received the Holy Ghost since you believed? And they said unto him, We have not so much as heard whether there be any Holy Ghost. [3]And he said unto them, Unto what then were you baptized? And they said, Unto

John's baptism. ⁴Then said Paul, John verily baptized with the baptism of repentance, saying unto the people, that they should believe on him who should come after him, that is, on Christ Jesus. ⁵When they heard this, they were baptized in the name of the Lord Jesus. ⁶And when Paul had laid hands upon them, the Holy Ghost came on them; and they spoke with tongues, and prophesied. Acts 19:2-6

Praying in tongues builds us up in our most holy faith; it is a strengthening agent for the believer. The Word of God also lets us know that praying in tongues is also for edification. Meaning when we pray in tongues there is a lifting of our spirits from the low place of humanity into the presence of God so that we can hear what He desires to say to us clearly. We no longer are confined to the realm of flesh but are propelled into the spirit, which is the place where the supernatural power we need resides. We pray in tongues as the Spirit of the Lord gives us utterance because there are things we know not to pray for but the Spirit of the Lord knows all things. Therefore when we pray we are praying the perfect will of God; His will, shall always prevail, which for us is a guaranteed victory in every area. Remember, He desires for us to prosper and be in health as our soul prospers. The more we pray, the stronger we become, and our spirits open to the God kind of prosperity. The more we open ourselves up for growth through dying to our resistance to the "dirty work" of the process for a life of Joy, the faster we will flourish and see our lives begin to transform.

THREE
WATERING YOUR JOY

He that believes on me, as the scripture has said, out of his belly shall flow rivers of living water. John 7:38

Naturally, one's body will not survive without water; all living substances require some degree of water to continue to function properly. As a result, you would continuously supply what's vitally needed for your survival and well-being because you want to ensure your health in that manner. Wouldn't you? I know that sometimes we have those moments when our bodies have started to tell us that we have begun to run low because we've gone too long without anything to drink and we experience being parched. Do you remember that very first sip after being extremely thirsty? The whole body responds to it, doesn't it? And all the way down, the refreshing phenomenon of water is felt. Because water has such an ability to heal and replenish it's one of life's most important necessities and is of the highest demand. In fact, 80% of our bodies contain water. Just as we require water naturally, spiritually we also require the same type of life-giving agent that prevents dryness. Being spiritually parched directly affects living a life of Joy. Your JOY needs to be replenished every day and refreshed consistently. Just as David of the Bible encouraged himself so must you. Out of your own belly, from your own lips, must be words that bring life into every situation. The Word of God declares that life and death are in the power of the tongue. Because out of your belly flows rivers of living waters it is solely your responsibility to filter what goes into your heart to ensure the purity of what comes out. For it is that which comes out of oneself that defiles oneself. Your words will either ignite blessings or curses into your life and those connected to you. In other words, within you lies a river with the potential to supply life or cause contamination.

The tongue has the power of life and death, and those who love it will eat its fruit. Proverbs 18:21

Beware of Contamination

Before we get to the good part of supplying life, let's deal with this contamination for a moment. Contaminates are self-destructive words, spiritual dryness caused by not praying, meditating or fellowshipping with other believers, and a lack of worship. You can very well cause your own contamination but the most subtle causes of contamination are usually found in the secrets of friendships or intimate relationships that are unequally yoked, words of discouragement spoken by those closest to your heart, or a decline in faith. They are classified as subtle because the underlining disdain for you is not as forthcoming and is designed to be unrecognizable without the use of discernment. Contaminates can slowly tear you down subconsciously and are hidden in: jokes, sly or quick remarks, sarcasm, automatic negative comments and lite persuasions of things you wouldn't normally do but may not necessarily be wrong to a degree. In other words, they have the potential to start bad habits which can lead to bondage when engaged in excessively. The effects of such do not seem to do much damage, at first sight, however, when accepted they can be your hindrance in allowing yourself to freely flow with what your faith desires to achieve. And because there is no flow watering your seed, your JOY withers. It takes the power of the Holy Spirit to sustain you, but it is your choice as to whether or not you are going to allow Him to flow through you to speak what God desires to happen in your life. It does not matter what's going on around you or where things look as though they are headed. All that matters is that you get to the water source and allow a free flow. "Free flow of what?" you may ask. A free flow of your faith: a free flow of speaking life into your hopelessness. This task is definitely a challenge because it forces us to ignore our senses. Most times we do not see positive, we do not hear positive nor do we feel positive when chaos has arrived. But, the moment you begin watering your JOY through the aid of the Holy Spirit you will begin to change right in the middle of that contaminated atmosphere.

Out of Your Belly

Notice I avoided saying you would change your contaminated atmosphere. I avoided saying such because before your atmosphere changes there must be a change in you. Out of your own belly, from your own spirit rivers of living water should flow. And in watering your Joy worship, praise and communion with God are your rivers. These three keep your Joy replenished and refreshed when done consistently. Personally, I call them the trinity of life because they are three in one with worship metaphorically being the Father, praise being the

Son and communion being the Holy Spirit. Each can stand independently but they are so closely connected that they can be considered as one. So we will do just that.

Many times we have become so susceptible to looking outward for stimulation or inspiration. It is almost as though when we have become dry we stand near others with flowing rivers with our beggar's cups stretched out hoping they would put a few drops in our cups. Have you noticed in the Body of Christ how we run from city to city, from conference to conference, musical to musical and event to event just for a drop in a cup? News Flash! You can produce what you are thirsty for, Out of Your Own Belly can flow rivers of living water. And worship is how you get there.

²³But an hour is coming and now is, when the true worshipers will worship the Father in spirit and truth; for such people the Father seeks to be His worshipers. ²⁴God is a spirit, and those who worship Him must worship in spirit and truth. John 4:23, 24

What is Worship?

Worship is so much more than singing a slow tempo song of admiration at a gathering. It is more than lifted hands, a bowed head or lying prostrate. Worship is a lifestyle, and it is a lifestyle that pays homage to God through the way that you live. In spirit and in truth is the requirement of true worship. Without the truth of God's word being operative in your life and the character of who He is being mirrored as a reflection through you, your worship is fake. Worship reaches for the heart of God. And in reaching for the heart of God we discover His nature. Genuine worship will never misplace its focus. What I mean by that is when you are worshipping God your focus should be Him and His will or pleasure only, and if at any moment that changes worship becomes invalid. Putting oneself in the spotlight automatically shifts God out of the spotlight. That may be a hard pill to swallow but I pray it also set you free from the lie that worship is all and only about a song. Living a lifestyle opposite of the nature of God will not allow access into the holiness of God's glory through worship regardless of if the singer can really sing and the melody sounds spiritual or not. There is such deception concerning what worship really is.

Creating a Flow

Worship in essence is your cleansing agent. Yes, the Word of God says that we "the church" are sanctified by the washing of water by the Word, but remember worship is done in spirit and in truth. Truth is the Word of God. So worship cleanses just as water also cleanses. Living a clean life modeled after the Word of God is indeed a life of worship.

When we allow God to create in us a clean heart and renew a right spirit within us worship has then shifted from something we do to who we are. So by there being a continuous flow of worshiping in your life you will not have a buildup of toxic residue. *It's nearly impossible to remain in a negative mood when true worship has emerged.* True Worship is worship without contamination, which is worship from a pure heart with a pure motive and mindset where loving God is the only focus, expels all negativity. True worship summons the presence of God; when His presence shows up His glory follows; when His glory shows up everything else bows.

I believe worship is under such an attack because through the watering of worship your seed of Joy is fed. Living a life of worship is no easy task, and is definitely not for the weak because it takes stamina and courage to stand for God in the midst of a culture that stands against Him. It takes sacrifice to decide to spend time at home in the presence of

God, it takes effort to consciously not participate in certain conversations, it takes a backbone to say, "NO as for me and my house we will serve God" and to begin to align your life in a manner that pleases God. But the benefits of being protected, provided for, and endowed with peace in the life of a true worshipper are immeasurable. The growth is exponential, but unless the seed is fed there can be no growth.

FOUR
Process of Growth

For we know that all things work together for good to them that love God, to them who are the called according to his purpose. Romans 8:28

For many years I'd heard this scripture, read it and even used it to encourage others. It had meaning to me at those times but it truly came to life when I began to understand what "to them" is really saying. I know we use the words "for them" a lot to prove a point but "to them" has a slightly different perspective of revelation that I believe we have yet to discover. For example, if I were to complete an assignment for you it is not the same as me presenting an assignment to you is it? Therefore, I'm inclined to believe that "all things work together for good to them" means the good and bad involve a type of process rather that transforms the individual inwardly. When we love God and are the called according to His purpose the things that happen around us are not working for us but are geared towards us to change us.

The Shift

If it works for good to you it gives us the choice or power to choose whether or not we are going to use the things presented to us for good or not. It has come your way for good but it is up to you to see the presentation as good, no matter what it looks like. Ever go through a moment of chaos where everything around you seemed to be crashing down all at the same time? Did not it all work out in the end? I do not know if you noticed or not but if you would take a moment to look back there was a definite turning point in the midst of the chaos that shifted things from worst to better. During those moments of chaos there comes a time when a decision must be made. That decision determines the timing of when everything will begin to work together for your good but after the bad has worked to push you into position. Remember the enemy means and sends chaos for your demise but God never wants you to be destroyed or defeated, He means all things for your good. Because He Loves YOU, Yes He Does!

So this, "working together for good to you" is a direct result of God being able to get a message through you to you. It's almost like a pruning process, yes it may hurt or be uncomfortable at the moment but it is all designed for your ultimate benefit. Look at it this way, most individuals who are great with money did not just wake up one day with the ability to handle money wisely. Instead many first became acquainted with experiencing poverty for a season. It was out of that experience that they learned how to manage, how to budget, prioritize and save. Those tough times can develop a sense of wisdom in us as we grow to realize what's truly important. The point is: during your season of hardship it may not feel or look as though things will work out! If you would stop for a moment and reflect on what you are learning during the process you will soon see that where you are now is not where you will always be.

You are growing!

Today we live in such a fast-paced society; everything is done so quickly and on the dime. We have the ability to access any type of information within seconds and at will. Unfortunately, in some areas, this has spoiled us because we tend to not want to wait for anything. And because growth is a process, impatience is almost inevitable, especially since the process of growth does not always happen quickly. Thus, impatience can become your enemy by causing you to delay your own process. I say that because impatience rarely allows one to receive properly because of anxiety. We already know that we are not to be anxious about anything. So along with that impatience are attached other character flaws that could cause you to step into error or out of timing. Impatience can cause frustration which leads to anger, anger leads to resentment, resentment leads to strife, or that same frustration can cause you to make a bad decision out of force because you have quickly become weary. We make some of our biggest mistakes thinking we are "making something happen" when moving too quickly out of frustration and impatience. While you are creating this false elevation you are merely prolonging the process because the greatness that God desires for you will not be reached through your own fleshly maneuvers. And since He is such a patient God He will keep you on that same cycle until you've decided to be willing to be processed into your growth. *There is usually an illusion of success that follows once an individual has broken away from their process of growth. In time it always shows because the success that they themselves have created never lasts. It always loses the strength of its joy.* This is why we cannot avoid the process of growth. We must be willing to be processed because it is our response that allows all things to work for our good.

The Process

Just as a seed has to be set in dirt in order for its shell to break for it to begin to grow, so are we when we find ourselves in the midst of challenging times. During the seed's discomfort, during the breaking of its shell it is growing. Many times we lack the capacity to acknowledge growth during moments of breaking because our discomfort overpowers our ability to process the growth that's taking place. We tend to recognize the more convenient encounters of growth - the less painful ones - but miss the lessons that spring forth through shell crushing moments. Growth develops in many different ways. However, in order for this process to begin there must be initiators of the process. The dirt around the shell provokes a response from the seed causing it to crack. The seed responds productively as a natural reaction. The dirt around you is designed to initiate your process of growth. Every time you find yourself in "dirt-like" situations that tend to feel as though they are squeezing or even suffocating you your litmus test for growth will be your initial response. You are growing when your emotions are noticeably changing, lifting, and are under control as a result of understanding some things may not feel good, but all things are necessary when working for your good. Having a revelation that causes you to focus your faith when life seems to be breaking you down is what propels your growth. Your shell is only being broken so that your roots can begin to establish themselves for your strength, stability, and later multiplication.

So what does all this mean? It means your shell, being things like material items, relationships, physical health or any other outward type of security that you have relied on, will sometimes go through moments of dirt. This dirt can be a loss, but it can also be a drastic change of some sort. Either way, the shell that you have been hidden in has to break to get to the core of who you are. Have you ever experienced a challenge that taught you something about yourself that you did not know was there? That was your shell breaking experience.

Reflection

Maybe this will help. I can remember a particular time when I had a massive crisis; ended up in the hospital for forty five days. Well during that time, it was truly a challenge. After my second time of coming off of the ventilator because my lungs had collapsed twice and my heart went into cardiac arrest I was having a very hard time recovering physically. Being on the ventilator was nothing new for me at that point; I had previously had numerous encounters with life support. Usually after coming off of the ventilator in a few days or a week at the most, I'm almost back to normal and am moving around. But not that time, that time two weeks had gone by and I still had not been able to walk. I was blind sighted by Paraplegia (paralysis) and it was in full effect. There was a moment when doctors were presenting me with options of going home in a wheelchair and having home health visits, after being placed in their extended stay program for three more months to do physical therapy for the rest of my body. Basically they were saying I would not be able to walk for another six months at a minimum. I could have chosen to accept the timeline of recovery and I think for a few hours I had, but then by the unction of the Holy Spirit my faith arose. I agreed to the physical therapy but refused to accept the fact that I would return home in a wheelchair. I kept saying, "I didn't roll in here, I walked in here, so I'm walking out", and I meant every word. During every therapy session I asked as many questions as I could think to remember. Then when I returned to my room I researched every answer on the internet to learn more about paralysis and extreme weaknesses as it related to myasthenia gravis and I secretly started my own therapy sessions right there in my room. Instead of sitting there watching television all day or playing on technical devices I went to work mentally, spiritually, and physically. Every hour on the hour I would try to move my legs and would speak to them while doing so. My friends would come to visit, some would try to get me to keep still (that was their last visit) and others would hold down one leg while I ferociously fought to lift the other (I kept them around). For a week nothing moved unless they moved it for me, but the second week there was a break through. I spilled a cup of ice that week and without thought as result of quickly reacting to the accident I lifted my leg on my own. It was hilarious! Isn't that ironic, I just needed a little ice to wake it up. One of my friends came from out of town to visit and while she was there I had an open vision of me walking again so I told her, "When I wake up in the morning I'm going to walk myself to the bathroom". That next morning I not only walked to the bathroom in my room, but I also surprised my nurse, who exploded into tears by walking all the way down the hall. Hospitals have long hallways ya know.

My growth took place at the moment of deciding to be tenacious in going to war against what was devastating me and putting it into use by pulling out of it the strength to push and fight until what I believed manifested. Many times we just accept the dirt around us rather than using it to strengthen us.

Tenacity is birthed during adversity.

When you've found yourself in a situation where the odds are against you, if you allow growth you'll discover your core is much stronger than you've paid attention to because it was hidden by so many outward insecurities that you built around it. I encourage you to instead allow the roots of your faith to begin to extend to areas far beyond what you have imagined you could ever reach or accomplish. For it is through the growth process that your roots become stabilized through the proven fortitude of your faith.

FIVE
The Root of JOY is Faith

*³Knowing this, that the trying of your faith worketh patience.
⁴But let patience have her perfect work, that ye may be perfect
and entire, wanting nothing.* James 1:3, 4

Many times when challenges arise, your faith can sometimes take the hardest blow, depending on the intensity and force of the opposition. Remaining or having to battle with the same struggles over a certain period of time can not only be draining, but it has the potential and many opportunities to discourage faith. Being discouraged in faith does not always mean that faith was not in operation. But the courage to believe what stimulated that faith has now been intimidated and its boldness has been bullied. There are trials with a specific assignment to uproot your faith, which then hinders your hope in what God promised He would do. The assignments are intentionally targeting your senses because oftentimes when your senses begin to experience an outcome that is contrary to a belief, it can begin to infect your belief like a bad grape in a bunch. Have you ever seen a cluster of grapes sit for too long? It may start out with just one grape that turned bad, but sooner than later, that whole bunch will turn bad, if you allow the bad grape to sit long enough it will infect the others nearby. The enemy uses this same tactic by implanting negativity through your senses. He tries to get you to allow a bad grape to sit by giving you a thought or negative feeling. The goal is for you to allow infection to take place instead of casting down the thoughts and imaginations that are contrary to the Word of God. *Your enemy is trying to spread doubt and unbelief.* Outwardly the magnitude of how unpromising things may be can be easily misconstrued by heightening the responses of your senses. Thus, causing you to focus on the unfavorable rather than believing all things are possible. Remember it's your faith that is the target here. So the objective of your enemy is to get you to abort every ounce of belief by any means necessary and since our senses are usually always our most vulnerable access points they are hit the hardest with negative sensations. If just one thought has come to mind like, "well maybe it really won't happen", your faith has just been attacked. These types of thoughts are almost guaranteed especially when you are standing in faith believing God for anything. The thought(s) the enemy attempts to plant will not be a successful implant if you disallow your senses to control what you think and believe. When your mind begins to have conflicting thoughts with your faith it's time to fight back with your other weapon, "your mouth". When your mind says you cannot your mouth should say you can, because it's out of the abundance of the heart that the mouth speaks and life and death are in the power of your tongue. There is power in your mouth, however if a thought remains long enough it matures into a way of living and will also affect your speech. It sounds much easier than it really is, especially considering times when there may be more than one opposing thought on your mind at one time. So beware of overwhelming thoughts. They may come but the good news is there are many answers to dealing with thoughts that continuously try to distract you from continuing in the mindset of victory found in the Word of God.

³For though we walk in the flesh, we do not war after the flesh: ⁴For the weapons of our warfare are not carnal, but mighty through God to the pulling down of strong holds; ⁵Casting down imaginations, and every high thing that exalts itself against the knowledge of God and bringing into captivity every thought to the obedience of Christ.

2 Corinthians 10:3-5

NOW Faith

Now faith is the substance of things hoped for, the evidence of things not seen. Hebrews 11:1

You cannot afford to allow your flesh to dictate your faith because the feelings of flesh tend to change with the temperature of the wind. But once faith has risen and taken root in your spirit it has the potential to become so strong that nothing can uproot it from the soil of your heart. NOW Faith is faith independent of your senses. It speaks of an active, current Faith that declares what has yet to manifest to the senses, but has already been completed in the spirit. For example, you may have lost your job and it looks as though you won't be able to make ends meet. In fact, the enemy may be trying to get you to think that God does not desire for you to prosper or that He will not supply your need, but Now Faith believes the scriptures that say, "God will supply all of your need according to His riches in glory", and that, "God wishes above all that you prosper and be in health as your soul prospers". (See Philippians 4:19, 3 John 1:2) You are actually given a choice at that moment to choose which truth you will believe: the truth of your flesh or the truth of your faith. *For the record, Faith always produces the greater outcome no matter how long it takes to pull into your life that which God has already said He desires for you to have.*

Unshakable Faith

The root of your joy is your faith and the strength of your faith is dependent upon the unshakeable, unmovable tenacity within your spirit and heart to believe God no matter what mirage of disappointment appears. The Word of God in your heart supplies the fertility of your soil. The Word creates an atmosphere of growth for faith to take root and go deeper and deeper, embedding and stabilizing you within, to be built to stand every test or storm that comes your way as you grow. When your Faith is in the Word of God and is, unshakable, you then become a threat to everything that has tried to discourage you because your Faith will produce the opposite. Your Faith provides depth to your Joy because believing God through adversities and uncertainties is your strength. When you think (there go those senses) you have no clue of how the outcome is going to turn out in your favor, your NOW Faith (which is your substance) knows exactly how everything will turn out. Because faith sees all things working together for the good of those who love God and are called according to His purpose. And Faith knows that because of intercession, when the enemy comes in like a flood, the Spirit of the Lord will raise up a standard against him. *Faith is not hoping: Faith is **convinced**!*

When your faith cannot be easily uprooted your Joy will not be easily disturbed.

SIX
THE BRANCHES OF JOY

For I know the thoughts that I think toward you, says the Lord, thoughts of peace, and not of evil, to give you an expected end. Jeremiah 29:11

During the process of growth, you have matured, you have increased in wisdom, your emotions are in check and you no longer toxify your life but have begun to feed your mind, body, and spirit properly. Now that you have grown a bit it's time to start reaching, stretching those branches towards your dreams and purpose. Everyone has a purpose; we were all created with intention. However, sometimes discovering your purpose may require a little more effort than anticipated. Discovering takes work but when you allow yourself to explore those hidden treasures inside you will notice there is much more to you than what meets the eye.

When we pause to look at a tree we see that its branches give its shape and identity, it allows outsiders such as yourself to witness the mold of its strength. The branches are what supply its beauty. Thus, in your life those areas that you've stretched out into, that new class you are going to decide to take, the football team that you are going to stretch out to start for inner city youth, or even the choice to strengthen your relationships, all make up your mold. They are the essences of what holds your true beauty. That is why knowing your purpose is so important but even if you don't know, stretching out into new arenas may help you in discovering it.

I strongly believe purpose is to be discovered not found. What I mean by that is your purpose is within you, therefore to know it requires you to come into an awareness of its existence rather than thinking your purpose has to be found, which implies a need for outsourcing. Truth is, your purpose is not lost and it cannot be stolen.

You may choose to forfeit the impact of your purpose by neglecting it, but it is still all yours. There may be moments of discouragement in discovering your purpose but I encourage you to not give up.

Discovery is the key and awareness is liberating.

For example, when a baby is born he is born with a pair of hands, but at the time he has not quite discovered the purpose of his hands, three months later he learns he can hold a bottle, as he develops mentally and physically he learns how to feed himself, as time progresses-how to tie a shoe, and later on how to repair a car. All along he was born with the perfect pair of hands but he did not initially have an understanding of their full purpose. Your capacity has to stretch to discover more for each stage and level in life. *You were born with everything that you need to live a life of Joy, your purpose is in your possession, just keep stretching and expanding your capacity to fulfill it.*

Reach for It

Purpose is often discovered inside your instinctual characteristics and passions. Teachers love knowledge, coaches love giving instructions, counselors are objective and entrepreneurs are innovative. Becoming aware of your natural characteristics helps you to navigate into your purpose. Most times when we find ourselves out of our element we become discontent and unfulfilled, which directly affects our Joy. Waking up every morning to a life lacking fulfillment can be quite frustrating especially when you know deep down that, "there must be more to life than this." The hope of wanting more but the lack of drive or inspiration to reach for more will always result in stagnation. If this sounds like your life right now do not be dismayed. Things can change and will change the moment you begin to stretch those branches. Start putting your faith to work! Do Something! By all means use wisdom but there is always something that can be done, even if it means coming up with a six-month plan to begin to do those things that are dear to your heart.

Branches facilitate the enhancements of your life. My mentor would say, "Success is turning out as God intended". So I'm saying the same to you. True Success in not determined by material objects but it is accomplished by fulfilling the intentions for which you were created. You were created to solve a problem. Even starting with a few small enhancements can make a difference, because they can catapult you into other more defining areas.

When I was dealing with depression because of my surgery scars and major weight gain (due to medication) I made a decision to begin to research losing weight. Following through started off as small, but made such an impact in my growth process. After losing one-hundred pounds I'm sure you can imagine how high my self-esteem was boosted! Not only that, but the confidence transferred into me believing that I could still Finish College. So, I went back to school to complete my degree. And while studying for my B.A. I also completed my School of Ministry coursework. But I did not stop there; once I started to grow emotionally, I grew mentally and spiritually simultaneously, while continuing to maintain physically. It was as if the more I allowed myself to grow by reaching for new areas to discover, the more I became liberated from the confines of what others thought I should remain in. If I had a dollar for every time someone told me "I couldn't or wouldn't be able to do something," I would be very wealthy right about now. But, "He, whom the Son has set free, is free indeed!"

So go ahead! Reach within yourself and expand yourself by enhancing what you've discovered within.

> **The key to expanding your branches and discovering your purpose is by reaching towards the SON.**

God lives in you and you in Him, for it is in Him that we live, move, and have our being. Again, Yes, He created you with and for a purpose, and because you were created "with" it, it's already in you, but you must get to Him to experience it! Who better to seek for counsel concerning what has been created than the creator? It just makes sense. As you continue to grow in God He will show you exactly who you are by leading you, because the steps of a God man are ordered by God. The closer you get to the sun the more we feel the effects of its rays, the closer we are to an individual the easier it is to recognize when they are speaking. Well, it is the exact same way with God, the closer you get to Him, the easier it becomes to recognize when He is speaking or not, and the easier it is to hear Him clearly when He speaks to guide you to your purpose. But guess what? Your purpose is not just for you.

SEVEN
THE FRUIT OF JOY

My Father is glorified and honored by this, when you bear much fruit, and prove yourselves to be My true disciples.

John 15:8

No one can tell you your full purpose but if you desire to live a transformed life, your God intended life of JOY, part of the essence of your purpose is to bear fruit and lots of it. The fruits of the spirit are love, joy, peace, longsuffering, gentleness, faith, goodness, meekness, and temperance. So what exactly is the fruit of Joy? Well, I'm glad you'd like to know. Do you remember our earlier conversation about what Joy is and how it is your strength? We spoke about how the Joy of the Lord is a direct result of your depth and stability; the ability to not be easily shaken or moved by external influences. So now you are in a position to bear fruit.

Unfortunately, so many times we see the process done out of order when individuals try to force fruit or produce ahead of the proper timing. There must be a proven growth process to be able to have the capacity to bear fruit. Fruit are quite beautiful to behold but they are not weightless, they require strength, that's if you expect to carry much. For example, starting a business without taking the time to learn your niche or an individual who may be called into ministry starting their own church without having taken the time to study properly or learn under the tutelage of another, both are attempting to bear fruit without branches. It's quite dangerous attempting to bear fruit without having the strength to withhold what's proclaimed. Oh, but when you are ready, Look out World!

But I have prayed for you, that your faith fails not: and when you are converted, strengthen your brethren. Luke 22:33

Each One Reach One

See, your growth was not just for you. Now it is time to reproduce after your own kind. It is time to teach others how to live a life of Joy, how to start their own business, improve their relationships, or start an organization they have been praying and preparing for.

Bearing fruit is not just about being able to feed others but it also perpetuates the ability to multiply. Within every fruit lies a seed(s) for the next generation of the same type of tree. Mentorship is the key to a stronger generation. One of my greatest desires, and I pray this becomes yours, is for my ceiling to be those that I mentor and my children's floor. Meaning because I know I will have taught them everything they need to know concerning being successful, fruitful and purposeful, they should be able to take off at my finishing point and continue my legacy of success to a greater degree. *I do not want them to be duplicates of me; I require them to be better than me.*

Being willing and open enough to allow someone else into your life to let them learn from you takes a lot of courage for most of us, especially when you have been hurt in the past. But the difference now is that you are wiser than before. You know how to discern the difference between good and bad fruit. Because your prayer life has increased you are stronger in your relationship with God and can hear Him clearly now when He says, "no, He's not the one, or just give her a bite of fruit (word of encouragement) but hold on to your seeds". *Everyone isn't meant to be intimately attached to you personally but anyone can be blessed by your life from a distance.*

When dealing with people we are to love everyone as Christ has commanded us to do so, however, we must not neglect the truth that everyone will not love us in return. With that being said just be mindful, but stay on course. Continue to give words of encouragement and as God leads you, plant seeds. By no means do you hide. Your Joy is supposed to be seen by the world. Oh taste and see that the Lord is Good! We are the salt of the earth and the light of the world. The way we identify a tree is by the fruit it displays, so now you are in a show and tell season. Go ahead; share the goodness of the Lord, through and by all means necessary! And while you are at it, make sure you are intentionally teaching someone else to do the same.

There is no greater feeling than the feeling of impacting someone else's life. It is such an awarding and humbling experience to be a part of someone else's process of progress. The favor of God always amazes me when I watch the lives of those who pour into the lives of others continuously; it is as if God supplies them with an unlimited grace and resources. The scriptures are unquestionably true. I guarantee it: I see it time after time.

¹Blessed is the one who does not walk in step with the wicked or stand in the way that sinners take or sit in the company of mockers, ²but whose delight is in the law of the Lord, and who meditates on his law day and night. ³That person is like a tree planted by streams of water, which yields its fruit in season and whose leaf does not wither whatever they do prospers. Psalm 1:1-3

EIGHT
Harvesting What's Yours

Give, and it shall be given unto you; good measure, pressed down, and shaken together, and running over, shall men give into your bosom. For with the same measure that ye mete withal, it shall be measured to you again. Luke 6:38

I know this scripture is used most in churches for offering inspiration but it is so much more and has a much greater reaching and meaning than the confinements of money. Let me explain.

Spoils of War

To harvest means to gather what you have reaped. During the Bible days after a war had been fought the winner would take their enemies captive and would do as desired with the spoils. The spoils were the lost and taken treasures of the defeated but the increased riches of the victors. The spoils became the right of the conquerors as a reward for winning another battle. Because war is never easy and often forces a warrior to fight until there is a guarantee of victory no matter what it takes after the war is over a celebration emerges in the camp of the victor.

Throughout this journey you have fought tooth and nail. You have fought the battles of your mind, the battles of training your flesh to pray and live a life of worship. You have fought the battles of faith when you chose to begin to be unmovable in believing God to do just as He promised in His Word. My friend, you have definitely defeated your enemies and you have done it well! It is now time to reap the spoils. All of the late nights and early mornings will pay off beginning today. Your harvest awaits! You have sown into Joy now its reaping season! All that you have sown into, whether it is your education, wisdom concerning finances, prayer life, relationship with God or others, encouraging words to others and anything else that you have given, it shall be given back to you in good measure. Because you have won!

Your last and final key to living a transformed life of Joy is by continuing in the vein of living a life of worship while allowing God to bring the increase. You have planted; you have watered; now it's His turn. And according to what He said, "He will cause men to give unto your bosom"; "He will make your enemies your footstool and will prepare a table before you in the presence of your enemies." (See Luke 6:38, Psalm 23:5, Luke 20:43) Sounds like harvest season to me!

Not only that but you will feast on a continual supply of Joy, love, peace, longsuffering, gentleness, meekness, faith and goodness. He will cause your hands to prosper and everything that you touch will be blessed. Remember to keep your soil fertile and free of contaminants. The more you reap and position yourself to reproduce, the more you will grow.

Congratulations on becoming a new perpetuator of a Life of

JOY!

"God Bless and Thank You for sharing your time with me"

Let us pray. Father, I thank You for my friend. I pray that they have received every word You have used me to sow into their life. I pray every word would begin to produce Joy during their present situation and continue on, beyond today, to bless their future as well. We decree that Everything that has held their Joy captive has released its grip and now a free flow of Joy has begun. Father Your word says that the anointing destroys the yoke, so we thank You for the destruction of depression, oppression, doubt, infirmity, affliction, and psychological and spiritual torment. We declare JOY shall remain and my friend shall continue to prosper as their soul prospers. We thank You for the wealth of wisdom that You have granted to us through …life of Joy and pray Your continuous favor and grace upon our lives as we share and sow into others. In Jesus Christ Name we give You glory and thank You for this privilege. **Amen**

SCRIPTURE REFERENCES

But my God shall supply all your need according to His riches in glory by Christ Jesus. Philippians 4:19

Beloved, I wish above all things that you may prosper and be in health, even as your soul prospers. 3 John 1:2

You prepare a table before me in the presence of my enemies. You anoint my head with oil; my cup overflows. Psalm 23:5

Give and it shall be given unto you; good measure, pressed down, and shaken together, and running over, shall men give into your bosom. For with the same measure that you mete withal, it shall be measured to you again. Luke 6:38

Till I make your enemies your footstool. Luke 20:43

[1]Blessed is the one who does not walk in step with the wicked or stand in the way that sinners take or sit in the company of mockers, [2]but whose delight is in the law of the Lord, and who meditates on his law day and night. [3]That person is like a tree planted by streams of water, which yields its fruit in season and whose leaf does not wither whatever they do prospers. Psalm 1:1-3

It is the spirit that quickens; the flesh profits nothing: the words that I speak unto you, they are spirit, and they are life. John 6:63

But we will give ourselves continually to prayer, and to the ministry of the word. Acts 6:4

²He said unto them, Have you received the Holy Ghost since you believed? And they said unto him, We have not so much as heard whether there be any Holy Ghost. ³And he said unto them, Unto what then were you baptized? And they said, Unto John's baptism. ⁴Then said Paul, John verily baptized with the baptism of repentance, saying unto the people, that they should believe on him who should come after him, that is, on Christ Jesus. ⁵When they heard this, they were baptized in the name of the Lord Jesus. ⁶And when Paul had laid hands upon them, the Holy Ghost came on them; and they spoke with tongues, and prophesied. Acts 19:2-6

He that believes on me, as the scripture has said, out of his belly shall flow rivers of living water. John 7:38

The tongue has the power of life and death, and those who love it will eat its fruit. Proverbs 18:21

²³But an hour is coming and now is, when the true worshipers will worship the Father in spirit and truth; for such people the Father seeks to be His worshipers. ²⁴God is a spirit, and those who worship Him must worship in spirit and truth. John 4:23, 24

For we know that all things work together for good to them that love God, to them who are the called according to his purpose. Romans 8:28

³Knowing this, that the trying of your faith worketh patience. ⁴But let patience have her perfect work, that ye may be perfect and entire, wanting nothing. James 1:3, 4

For I know the thoughts that I think toward you, says the Lord, thoughts of peace, and not of evil, to give you an expected end. Jeremiah 29:11

Now faith is the substance of things hoped for, the evidence of things not seen. Hebrews 11:1

My Father is glorified and honored by this, when you bear much fruit, and prove yourselves to be My true disciples. John 15:8

But I have prayed for you, that your faith fails not: and when you are converted, strengthen your brethren. Luke 22:33

These things have I spoken unto you, that my joy might remain in you, and that your joy might be full. John 15:11

"A picture is worth a thousand words, as is a testimony is worth a thousand scriptures." SELAH

Life of JOY by QuiNina J. Sinceno
www.quininaj.com

Email: only1paradigm@gmail.com

Social Media: @QuiNinaJ #ParaDigm @QuiNinaJSinceno

www.ingramcontent.com/pod-product-compliance
Lightning Source LLC
Chambersburg PA
CBHW072057290426
44110CB00014B/1717